UFOs

UNIDENTIFIED
FLYING OBJECTS

UNIDENTIFIED FLYING OBJECTS

by Howard Liss

Hawthorn Books, Inc.   Publishers   New York

To my daughters, Jodi and Dana,
who I hope will someday reach the stars

UNIDENTIFIED FLYING OBJECTS

Copyright © 1968 by Howard Liss. Copyright under International
and Pan-American Copyright Conventions. All rights reserved, including the right to reproduce this book or portions thereof in any
form, except for the inclusion of brief quotations in a review. All
inquiries should be addressed to Hawthorn Books, Inc., 260 Madison
Avenue, New York, New York 10016. This book was manufactured in
the United States of America and published simultaneously in Canada
by Prentice-Hall of Canada, Limited, 1870 Birchmount Road, Scar-
borough, Ontario.

Library of Congress Catalog Card Number: 68-27653

ISBN: 0-8015-8190-7

4 5 6 7 8 9 10

CONTENTS

1

WHAT ARE UFOs?

The letters UFO are an abbreviation for the words "Unidentified Flying Object."

For many centuries man has seen strange moving objects in the skies. There are accounts of flaming clouds, or balls of fire, moving across the heavens at great speeds. Most of the time these objects have remained aloft, hovering in one spot for a short time before moving out of sight. But sometimes, eyewitnesses have said, one of these weird vehicles has landed on the Earth, and strange creatures have come to visit us.

One of the earliest stories of a UFO landing is to be found in the Bible (Book of Ezekiel). It tells of a whirlwind that came out of the north. At first it appeared as a great cloud of fire, but as it landed the object took the shape of a wheel.

From this wheel came four living creatures. Each one had four faces, four wings, the hands of a man, and the feet of a calf. The four faces included one of a man, one of a lion, a third of an ox, and the fourth was that of an eagle.

Since that time there have been numerous sightings. In the year 583 A.D. Gregory of Tours, the first historian of France, wrote of globes of fire moving across the heavens. In 1478 a ball of fire was seen traveling over the mountains of Switzer-

An artist's interpretation of Ezekiel's vision.—*New York Public Library*

land. Other sightings of luminous balls have been reported in newspapers in the years 1871, 1881, and 1889. They told of spiraling objects, seen over Europe, Canada, Turkey, and New Zealand.

Not all the sightings have taken the form of fiery globes. In the year 1873 a number of people in the town of Bonham, Texas, saw a huge, silvery, cigar-shaped "flying machine." Moving swiftly and silently, it flew around the town twice and then disappeared. Of course, the sighting took place many years before the airplane had been invented.

The next day a similar flying machine was observed by people in Fort Scott, Kansas.

In 1926 a team of American explorers, led by Nicholas Roerich, saw a UFO as they were traveling through Mongolia. It was a huge, circular object seemingly made of a silver-grey metal, and it streaked southward for a few seconds, then suddenly veered to the southwest and was gone from view.

Since World War II there have been thousands of additional sightings in various parts of the world.

Some people are convinced that these UFOs are really spaceships, coming to Earth from another planet, or perhaps from as far away as a star. Other people say that there are no such things as spaceships which can come from outer space, and that the earthly origins of all UFOs can be scientifically explained.

Are the UFOs really visitors from other worlds? Is there life somewhere in outer space? Is a trip from distant stars possible? Or, are these UFOs merely natural phenomena?

Read on and decide for yourself!

2

SIGHTINGS FAR AND WIDE

On June 24, 1947, an air search party was organized to hunt for a marine transport plane that had supposedly crashed in the Cascade Mountains of Washington. One of the searchers was Kenneth Arnold, who owned his own small plane and often flew to various cities on business trips.

The marine plane was not found and, after searching for about an hour, Mr. Arnold decided to continue on toward the city of Yakima.

The air was smooth, the sun was shining, and Mr. Arnold leaned back in his seat to enjoy the beautiful scenery. He had flown for only a few minutes after giving up the search, when suddenly he saw a bright light reflected on his plane.

Looking toward his left, he saw a chain of nine circular objects, about twenty-five miles from his own plane. The objects were flying in formation toward Mt. Rainier, the highest mountain in the Cascades. They swerved through the other high mountains, streaking along the snow-covered ridges at a great rate of speed, with the sun glinting off their silvery, metallic sides. Mr. Arnold estimated that the objects were traveling at the rate of 1,656 miles per hour!

When Kenneth Arnold landed at Yakima, he told his story to the newspapers.

That same day a prospector named Fred Johnson was in the Cascade Mountains. He noticed several objects in the sky exactly like those seen by Kenneth Arnold. Using his telescope, he followed the movements of these "flying saucers" for a few seconds before they disappeared. The prospector also noticed that while the UFOs were passing, the magnetic needle of his compass moved about in a peculiar fashion, for no apparent reason.

On January 7, 1948, many residents of Madisonville, Kentucky, called the state police. They reported that a huge, round object was hovering over the town, giving off a bright red glow.

The state police called the military police of Fort Knox, located about one hundred miles away. The military police called nearby Godman Air Force Base. And, a short time later, officers and crew in the tower of the base spotted the UFO.

Colonel Guy Hix, the base commander, knew that a squadron of P-51 fighter planes was being ferried to another air base near Louisville, Kentucky. He knew that those planes were still in the air. He contacted the leader of the squadron, Captain Thomas Mantell, Jr., and asked him to investigate.

The P-51 is not a jet plane; it is propeller-driven, and quite slow by modern standards. Yet it was capable of flying at least 360 miles per hour. The pilots were confident that they could catch the object, or at least find out what it was.

There were four planes in the squadron. One of them did not take part in the search for there was no oxygen in this aircraft, and the pilot dared not climb to high altitudes. The other three began the investigation.

Suddenly, Captain Mantell's voice came over the radio. He said, "I am closing in now to take a good look. It is directly ahead of me and moving at about half my speed. The thing looks metallic and of tremendous size."

Mantell continued to report that the object seemed to "rest" for a few seconds, then pick up speed again. It always managed to stay ahead of the surging P-51.

Finally, Captain Mantell's voice was heard again: "It's going up now and forward as fast as I am. That's 360 miles per hour. I'm going up to 20,000 feet. If I can't get closer, I'll abandon the chase."

Those were the last words heard from Captain Thomas Mantell. About an hour later, searchers found his crashed plane. He had hit the ground with such great force that the wreckage was strewn over more than half a mile. Examination of the bits and pieces of the plane revealed that the left wing must have broken off.

There was one other odd fact. Captain Mantell had contacted Godman Tower for the last time at fifteen minutes past three. When the searchers found him, they saw that his wrist watch had stopped at eighteen minutes past three.

On April 24, 1964, at five-thirty in the afternoon, police officer Lonnie Zamora went racing through the town of Socorro, New Mexico. He was chasing the driver of an automobile who had broken the local speed limit.

The speeder turned into a dead-end street. Officer Zamora stopped his police car and waited, knowing that sooner or later, the lawbreaker had to come out the same way.

Suddenly, the police officer heard a loud roar. It came from a gully in a deserted section west of town. Zamora knew that nobody lived in that area, which was just a piece of desert covered with sagebrush. But he realized that there was an old dynamite shack there and thought that someone had accidentally blown it up. There was dust flying all over the scrub plants.

Officer Zamora drove up a bumpy road to the top of a hill,

forgetting about the speeder, for the strange uproar seemed to warrant immediate investigation. He got out of his car and looked around.

About half a mile away, he saw a white, egg-shaped object lying in the gully. At first he thought it might be a car which had crashed and was standing on end.

He also saw two figures standing beside the object. He could not see what they looked like, except that they appeared to be wearing white overalls. The figures seemed to be about four feet tall.

The police officer went back to his car and radioed the information to his headquarters. He said that he would investigate further.

Zamora then drove along the bumpy road until he was about one hundred yards from the object. It was still in the gully, but the figures were no longer to be seen. Now he could see that it was indeed egg-shaped and about the size of a car. Its surface was white and smooth, without any windows.

There was another roar from the "egg," and officer Zamora dashed for the protection of some bushes, thinking the object was going to explode. Instead, however, the "egg" rose straight up about twenty feet off the ground and hovered. Looking up at it, Zamora could see red markings, something like letters, on one of its sides.

The object remained hovering for a few seconds, then flew away along the gully and disappeared. Officer Zamora ran back to his car and tried to radio his headquarters again but found that his radio was not working.

It took some time before the radio went on again. When it did, Zamora called the New Mexico State Police. He told them what he had seen. They sent Sgt. Sam Chavez to join Zamora.

The two officers went down into the gully where the object

had been. The sagebrush and mesquite were still smouldering, as if they had been burned by some sort of fire or heat. There were imprints in the ground; officer Zamora had noticed that the object was standing on "legs" before it rose up and flew away.

Sgt. Chavez called the U.S. Army to help explain the mystery. Some engineers with Geiger counters came and searched the ground for signs of radioactivity. They could find nothing.

On September 3, 1965, eighteen-year-old Norman Muscarello was walking on Routs 150. He had been hitchhiking from Amesbury, Massachusetts, to his home at Exeter, New Hampshire. It was two o'clock in the morning. There were no cars on the road and only a few houses looming up in the dark, moonless night.

Suddenly, a huge, glowing object came gliding silently toward him across the fields. The youth was terrified and leaped into a ditch. He watched as the object glided over a house, its red lights pulsing. Young Norman estimated that it was about eighty feet wide!

As the object backed away from the house, Norman ran to another house nearby and pounded on the door frantically. But the occupants, thinking he might be a robber, would not let him in. Norman raced along the road until he came to still another house but did not stop, for he realized it would be useless to pound on a stranger's door in the middle of the night. They would surely keep the door locked. He saw a car coming down the road and sprinted over to it. The people in the car listened to his story and drove him to the police station at Exeter.

The police officer in the station told Norman to go back to the area where he had seen the object. Patrolman Eugene

Bertrand was assigned to take him there in a police car.

When officer Bertrand heard Norman's story, he told the other officer that the boy's story must be true, for he had come upon a parked car on a different road. In the car was a very frightened woman. She said that she too had seen this glowing object with the pulsing red lights. In fact, it had followed her car for about nine miles, coming within a few feet of her before going away.

The police officer and the youth returned to the field. At first they could see nothing. Officer Bertrand shone his powerful flashlight through the trees trying to find out if the object was still there. Some distance away the boy and the policeman saw a corral where some farm horses were kept. They walked toward the corral fence and, as they trudged across the field, officer Bertrand thought to himself that perhaps the mysterious UFO was really a helicopter. But when he mentioned this to Norman, he was told that it certainly was *not* a helicopter.

Suddenly, the horses began to whinny in fright. Dogs at houses in the vicinity set up a fearful barking. And young Norman Muscarello, looking through the trees, shouted, "I see it!"

The huge object rose silently from behind some tall pine trees. The field and the few surrounding houses were bathed in red light as the UFO wobbled soundlessly toward them.

"I see it too!" shouted officer Bertrand. For an instant he thought of firing at the object with his service revolver but decided against it. Instead, he grabbed Norman's arm and pulled him toward the police car.

As they reached the car, another police automobile pulled up. It was driven by police officer David Hunt, and he too saw the huge UFO with the pulsing red lights.

As the two officers and the young man watched, the object flew away and was lost from view.

When the Air Force was notified of the incident, they admitted that they had been conducting an operation which they called "Big Blast." Some of their large B-47 airplanes had been practicing nighttime refueling in the air and had also been assigned to photographic missions from low altitudes. The Air Force planes were equipped with flashing red lights. But Operation Big Blast had been completed. There were no military planes in the air in that area after one-thirty in the morning. Norman Muscarello had seen the UFO at two o'clock, and the police officers saw it much later.

Presque Park Peninsula is located near Erie, Pennsylvania. In August, 1966, sixteen-year-old Betty Jean Klem and her boyfriend, nineteen-year-old Douglas Tibbetts, were sitting in a car at Presque Park. The wheels of the automobile were hopelessly stuck in the sand, and they were waiting for another car to come along and pull them out.

They say that they saw a "machine" in the sky. It seemed to have five sides and many lights along the sides. They were very frightened when the machine landed about one hundred yards from them.

At this point an officer in a cruising police car, noticing the flashing tail lights of Tibbetts's car, went to investigate. When the police officer heard the young couple's story, he and Douglas Tibbetts decided to investigate. They walked toward the spot where the object had been seen, but they saw and heard nothing.

Betty Klem had remained in the car. Looking out the window, she saw a "shapeless thing" approaching, and she pressed down on the horn again and again. The policeman and Betty's boyfriend came running back quickly. But they saw nothing.

Later, Air Force Major William Hall went to Presque Park Peninsula to check on the story. He moved about the sand looking for some sign of the "thing."

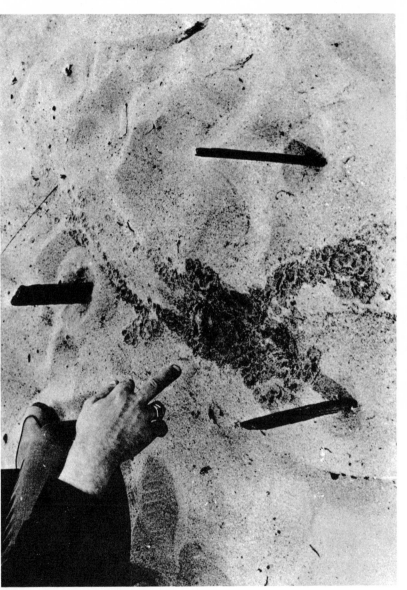

This formation, possibly a clawprint, was found in the sand near a UFO sighting.—*UPI*

Not far from the spot where Tibbetts's car had been stuck, he found the imprint of a kind of giant claw. When asked about it later, Major Hall would say nothing more.

There have also been many sightings in countries other than the United States and quite a few at sea.

During the International Geophysical Year 1957-1958, scientists from all over the world took part in various experiments intended to increase the knowledge of mankind.

Brazil converted one of its naval training ships into a kind of "floating laboratory." The Brazilian ship was sent six hundred miles into the South Atlantic to conduct a variety of experiments.

On February 21, 1958, a Brazilian Air Force officer, who happened to be standing on deck, suddenly shouted out, *"Olha o disco!"* (A flying saucer!)

A photographer happened to be close by. He had his camera with him and it was loaded with film. The photographer managed to take six pictures of the UFO before it disappeared. It took less than half a minute to take the pictures.

The photographer, whose name was Almiro Barauna, developed the film when the ship returned to Brazil. He made a number of prints and enlargements and gave them to the Brazilian Navy. They were shown to President Juscelino Kubitschek who turned them over to the newspapers.

There has been no further explanation.

These are only a few of the sightings which have never been explained. They puzzle scientists, who cannot offer reasons for the objects' presence. Were they really spaceships from other worlds?

3

SOME EXPLANATIONS

The vast majority of UFO sightings can be explained. Sometimes it may take several years before simple reasons are found for the sighting of a set of lights or silvery objects in the sky.

In August of 1951 three men gathered in a backyard in Lubbock, Texas. They were looking up at the sky. There had been many "shooting stars" that night and they were having fun trying to count them.

The men were all college professors at Texas Tech: Dr. W. I. Robinson, a geology teacher; and Professor W. L. Ducker and Dr. A. G. Oberg, both of whom taught engineering.

As they watched the skies, they saw about fifteen or twenty yellow-white lights passing overhead. A short time later another group of lights, similar to the first group, moved silently through the night. A few minutes before midnight, still another group of the lights glided by.

All three professors judged that the lights were about fifty thousand feet high and were traveling at a speed of approximately eighteen thousand miles per hour. They telephoned the local newspaper and told what they had seen.

A few days later, a young man named Carl Hart, Jr., who also lived in Lubbock, saw the same kind of lights. He grabbed his camera, ran into the yard, and took pictures of the strange objects.

At first, even the Air Force could not explain what those lights were. To them it was a mystery, along with many others of a similar nature which they could not solve.

The professors, however, did not give up so easily. They kept experimenting, trying to see if perhaps they could make similar lights appear again. They poked about through the town, hoping that something would turn up which might give them a clue. At last they found the answer.

The town of Lubbock had installed some new, powerful mercury vapor lights on one of their downtown streets. When flights of migrating plovers flew overhead, the strong lights from the street reflected on their white, oily breasts and caused the mysterious flying lights overhead. Scanning the lights with strong binoculars, one of the professors could even see the birds' feet.

They were not flying at an altitude of fifty thousand feet, but only at one thousand feet. They were not flying at eighteen thousand miles per hour, but only at fifty miles per hour.

The professors realized that perhaps their own imaginations had played tricks on them. They had been looking at "shooting stars," which were very high in the heavens. They had probably thought the strange lights were also quite high up. It is an established fact that it is very difficult to estimate the altitude and speed of an object at night, especially when the size of the object is not known.

Yes, even college professors can make mistakes!

On July 19, 1952, at around midnight, a number of blips appeared on the radar screens of the Civil Aeronautics Administration Air Route Traffic Control Center in Washington, D.C. They seemed to be traveling at a speed of slightly more than one hundred miles per hour. Moreover, the objects seemed to be acting in a peculiar fashion. One of them even started to reverse its direction without first stopping and then turning around.

A commercial plane took off to investigate. Soon the pilot saw a round light. He was about to report to the Traffic Center when suddenly the light gathered speed and disappeared. At the same time it vanished from the radar screens of the Center.

For a period of ten days, reports of UFOs around Washington continued to pour into the Control Center. Finally, the Air Force presented the explanation.

On July 19, Washington was suffering a "temperature inversion."

A temperature inversion is quite common in many areas and is caused when a layer of cold air is sitting on top of a layer of warm air. Normally, warm air rises and cold air sinks to the ground. So the warm air should have been on top of the cold air.

Radar waves can cause "illusions"—things that are not really there. The blips on the radar screen were "ghost blips" which were caused by the temperature inversion. In a temperature inversion the air is "disturbed" and radar waves were bouncing off the disturbances.

There are several radar experts and other technicians who do not agree with this explanation, but the Air Force has maintained that the temperature inversion was responsible for the blips and the sightings.

In 1966, the state of Michigan was the scene of UFO sightings for three consecutive days: March 19, 20 and 21.

On March 19, the town of Milan was lit up by a glowing object. County Police Sgt. Nuel Schneider and Deputy David Fitzpatrick went to investigate. They saw three bright objects and took pictures of them. The objects looked like tops turned upside down. The officers watched the glowing objects from two o'clock in the morning until seven o'clock, a total of five hours.

The next night glowing objects were sighted in the swampy area near Dexter, a town about sixteen miles from Milan. A dozen policemen and many other people saw the lighted objects. One policeman said that a glowing object flew over the top of his car as he was driving toward the swamp.

A man and his son ran to a spot about five hundred yards from the glowing object. They said that it was about the size of a car and shaped like "an oversized football."

The object suddenly rose from the ground, making a loud popping noise. Others, who said they also heard the sound of the object rising, said it was "like the echo of a ricochetting bullet." Policemen also reported hearing that same sound.

More lighted objects showed up the following night, this time at the college town of Hillsdale, located about forty-five miles from Dexter. Many girl students at Hillsdale College and some other people watched the glowing objects for almost four hours. These too were in a swamp. The objects seemed to change colors. And again the description was the same— the lights looked like oversized footballs.

The explanation was supplied by Dr. J. Allen Hynek, an astrophysicist from Northwestern University.

Those UFOs were just swamp gas (sometimes also called fox-fire or will o' the wisp).

The scientist said that rotting vegetation in a swamp produces gas, which is trapped in the swamp by ice and other cold winter conditions. In March a warm spell had suddenly melted the ice. The luminous gas was released. Such gas always makes a popping noise.

Dr. Hynek also pointed out that if those lighted objects were really space ships, they would hardly select a swamp as a good landing field.

There are some people who do not agree with the explanation offered by the scientist. But there are a great many more who do, for Dr. Hynek is one of the most respected scientists in the United States.

On September 5, 1962, glowing objects were seen throughout parts of the United States and Canada. The area included Ontario, Canada, and parts of the states of Iowa, North and South Dakota, Minnesota, Wisconsin and Michigan.

The crew of an airplane flying over Duluth, Minnesota, was the first to report the UFOs. They described them as bright and circular. Suddenly the objects broke into pieces. Each piece had a glowing red tail.

A few minutes later, the crew of a plane flying over Minneapolis, Minnesota, saw a UFO. It too was round, bright, and had a red tail.

Other people in the Midwest reported seeing objects that were quite similar. All, they said, went streaking through space silently.

It was almost five o'clock in the morning when some police officers in the town of Manitowoc, Wisconsin, came upon a large piece of metal lying in the street. It looked like a piece of slag from a foundry, and the officers thought it had dropped from a passing truck.

The answer to the mystery was soon supplied by the U.S. Government. That chunk of metal was actually part of Russia's Sputnik IV.

When the Russian Government had sent the space vehicle

Sputnik IV aloft, scientists calculated that the four-ton craft would stay in orbit for approximately 543 days. It was due to come down at any time from September 4 to September 6. Most likely the friction of the metal rubbing against the atmosphere would cause the Sputnik to burn up in the skies. And most of it did burn, for the chunk that reached Earth was all that was left. None of the scientists had thought that any of the pieces would survive the trip down through the atmosphere.

The piece of metal was thoroughly examined by the Milwaukee Astronomical Society. They proved that it had been out in space, about one hundred to two hundred miles up.

Thus a UFO—Unidentified Flying Object—became an IFO—Identified Flying Object.

On December 15, 1966, a pilot was taking some samples of air over Death Valley, California, and saw some green lights moving through the sky. He guessed that their altitude was about fifty thousand feet. Two other planes, which were nearby, also saw the green lights.

As they were reporting the sighting, a voice came over the radio. It was a technician at Tonopha, Nevada, Air Force Station.

"We sent those objects up," he said. "What you are seeing is green fluorescence—aluminum trimethyl. We are in the midst of an experiment studying wind currents.

"Those lights are not fifty thousand feet up," he added. "They are four hundred thousand feet up!"

It proved anew how the human eye can mislead even experienced observers, and how difficult it is to judge the altitude of an object without scientific instruments.

These are only a few examples of UFOs which have been explained to the satisfaction of most people.

A number of other scientific explanations have been offered to show that many UFOs are not really spaceships at all. One theory was given by a man named Philip Klass. Mr. Klass graduated from Iowa State with a degree in electrical engineering and later became Avionics Editor (avionics means the use of electric or electronic devices in aviation) for a highly respected magazine called *Aviation Week and Space Technology*. He thinks that many UFOs are really ball lightning.

Ball lightning is not completely understood by scientists, but they have observed it. They think it is a ball of electrified gas, sometimes measuring five feet in diameter. It glows in space, just as a UFO would glow.

Many stories of UFOs have also been elaborate practical jokes.

One of the most famous of all UFO photographs was taken in 1947 by a photographer named Bert Ruoff, who worked for Armco Steel Co. He was taking pictures of the blast furnaces of Hamilton Steel Co. in Hamilton, Ohio, and did not notice what was on his film until he developed it.

His pictures showed a number of bright lights glowing all around the blast furnaces. But, actually, the lights were the result of trick photography, producing an optical illusion. His camera had one concave and one convex lens (each lens was curved in the opposite direction). Anyone who had photographed those furnaces, with the same kind of camera and with the lights placed at exactly the right angle, could have produced exactly the same picture.

Yet many American newspapers believed Mr. Ruoff when he said that he could not explain what the lights were. They printed the picture. Other papers in Germany, Australia, and South Africa believed his photographs might be UFOs and they also printed the pictures.

Bert Ruoff enjoyed the joke for twenty years. Finally, he confessed that it was all in fun.

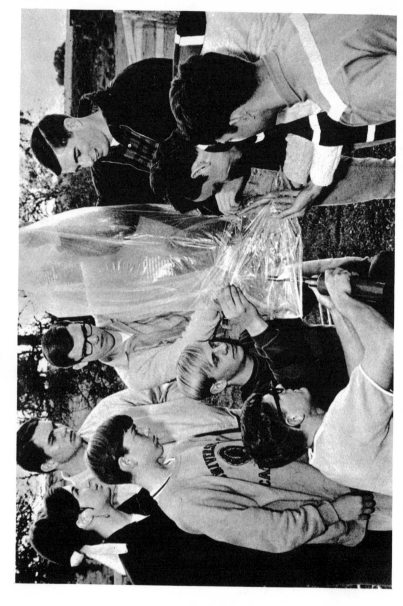

Sacramento, California, high school students show how they made a "flying saucer" from a plastic laundry bag, a crossbrace, and candles.—*UPI*

On December 3, 1966, a California highway patrolman radioed to his headquarters that he had sighted a "flying platform." It seemed to be well-constructed because it had "struts" —rods which were bracing the sides. It glowed faintly and was about the size of a hot-water heater. Most curious of all, there seemed to be a creature inside wearing a crash helmet.

It took four days for the truth to come out. The flying platform was the work of a high-school junior named Jon Barnard. When asked later exactly what he had built, the young man explained: His type of flying platform was constructed from a plastic bag—the type commonly used by cleaning stores to protect suits and dresses—plus some plastic soda straws and a few candles.

He taped up the top of the plastic bag, through which the coat hanger had been poked. The "struts" were plastic soda straws. Additional straws were inserted, end to end, and they served as a kind of candlestick on which the lighted candles were placed.

He lit the candles and allowed hot air to fill the plastic cleaning bag. The hot air made the plastic bag rise. The candles provided the glow. And there was nobody inside wearing a crash helmet. That was something the police officer only imagined he saw.

On December 3, 1966, Jon Barnard sent up thirty of those "flying platforms." Only one of them was reported.

When Jon's father found out about the practical joke, he said firmly, "There won't be any more of them!"

4

HUMANOIDS
FROM OUTER SPACE

The word "humanoid" is not found in many dictionaries. But books about UFOs and almost all science fiction stories use the word to describe creatures who have a resemblance to human beings.

There are a number of people all over the world who claim that they have not only seen spaceships zooming through the skies, but also that they have watched the ships land on Earth and observed the occupants of those ships get out and stroll around.

Sometimes the people watching these creatures have become frightened and run away. At other times the UFO occupants apparently became frightened, returned hurriedly to their spaceships, and streaked back into the heavens. But a surprising number of people stubbornly maintain that they have spoken to the creatures and, indeed, had many different experiences with them.

What did these humanoids look like? Well, there have been all sorts of descriptions.

Some humanoids look exactly as we do, being smaller or as tall as we are, or even much taller. A few have been described as resembling monkeys, except that they do not have monkey faces. They are said to have been seen running about on all fours. There are reports of humanoids with lots of hair on their bodies and pumpkin-shaped heads. Some of the creatures walked sideways, others floated, a few flew. There have been tales of humanoids whose skin glowed, or whose skin was very pale, or very dark. Humanoids are strong, say some who have encountered them. Humanoids are not strong at all, others claim.

In most cases the creatures seem to be wearing some kind of metallic coveralls to protect their bodies, and often they wear clear plastic helmets on their heads, perhaps to allow them to breathe the kind of air they are accustomed to.

There have been stories that humanoids are not the only occupants of these spacecraft. Robots accompany them.

Are the creatures friendly? Are they hostile? Witnesses can be found who will say that they have been attacked by the robots and almost killed. Others say that the humanoids (not the robots) are friendly folk and have even given a few fortunate Earth people a nice ride in their spaceships.

A man named Daniel Fry tells of encountering a landed spacecraft in the desert near White Sands, New Mexico. He was not afraid of it, but when he reached out his hand to feel what the craft was made of, a voice from out of nowhere told him, "Don't touch the hull, it's hot."

Since there was no crew on the landed ship, Mr. Fry reasoned that the voice must have come from a "mother ship" that was hovering somewhere.

Mr. Fry was invited to go aboard and he did. The craft took off and flew from White Sands to New York City and back again, a distance of almost five thousand miles, in about half an hour.

By comparison with some others, Mr. Fry's ride was a very short one. A farmer named Buck Nelson claimed that he had been given trips to the moon, to Venus, and to Mars!

Many of the stories are much alike. Eyewitnesses say that a spaceship lands and humanoids get out. A large proportion of them are small, perhaps three feet tall. Often they make strange sounds, gutteral noises, crackling chatter like geese, or some other kind of "speech" which is not understood. Some people, however, say the humanoids spoke to them in the language of the country where they landed. Still others maintain that they were able to establish communication through "mental telepathy" or thought waves. Sooner or later, in most of these accounts, the humanoids return to their ships and fly away, and nothing very much has happened to the human beings involved.

This was *not* the case when Barney Hill and his wife, Betty, made contact with humanoids. The incident took place on September 19, 1961. A book titled *The Interrupted Journey* has been written about their strange experience.

Betty and Barney Hill were returning from a Canadian vacation, driving along Route 3 in New Hampshire, heading for their home in Portsmouth. It was a bright night with a full moon and many stars gleaming brightly in the heavens.

As they drove, Betty Hill noticed a bright star near the moon, one she had not seen previously. Later, when the car was stopped so that the Hill's pet dachshund, Delsey, could take a short walk, Betty Hill looked at the star through binoculars. It seemed to be moving closer to Earth.

As they resumed the journey, Betty Hill kept looking at the moving light, and soon she and her husband realized that it wasn't a star or satellite, but a kind of brightly lighted object. There were also flashing lights rotating around the object, colored red, amber, green, and blue. The UFO made no sound.

As it continued to come closer, the craft seemed to be head-

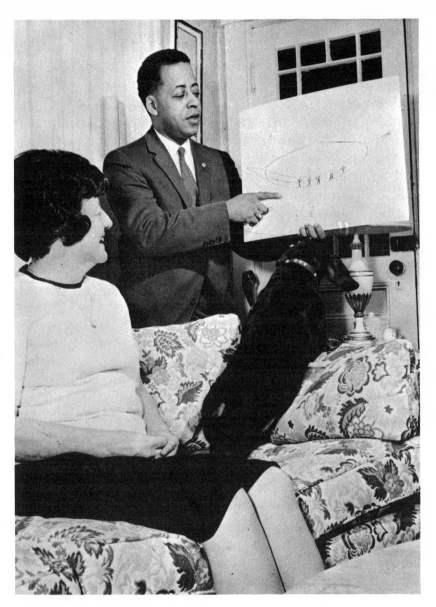

Barney and Betty Hill explain the flying saucer which they say abducted
them.—*UPI*

ing directly toward the car. Delsey, the dachshund, lay whining and cowering on the floor. The UFO kept pace with the car and even slowed down so the Hills were able to get a better look at it. Now they could see that it had double rows of windows.

Barney Hill stopped the car and got out so that he could see the UFO more clearly. He left the engine running and ran into the field toward the ship, which was now hovering at treetop level. When he was fifty feet away he stopped. Betty Hill called to her husband, but he did not answer her.

With his binoculars, Barney Hill could clearly see six humanoids looking at him from the windows. One, who seemed to be the leader, wore a black leather jacket.

Now the ship lowered some kind of fins to which red lights were attached.

Barney Hill was frightened. He seemed to sense that he would be captured and ran back to the car. He got in and sped away. Betty Hill looked back toward the ship. It was gone.

Moments later they heard a strange beeping noise coming from behind the car. Betty and Barney Hill both felt very drowsy.

It seemed only a short time afterward that they heard the beeping sound again. Looking out the car window, they saw that they were approaching the town of Concord. They arrived home in Portsmouth at five o'clock in the morning.

Several things bothered Betty and Barney Hill. First, there were some shiny spots on the trunk of the car, each about the size of a half dollar. Later, Betty tried an experiment with a compass. When she held it near the front or sides of the car, the compass acted normally; when she placed it on one of the shiny spots, the compass needle swung around wildly.

Second, Barney Hill found that the tops of his best and

newest shoes, which he had worn on the drive home, were badly scuffed. He reasoned that the only way the shoes could have been damaged in such a fashion was to have dragged them over some rocks.

Third, neither Betty nor Barney Hill could remember having driven from Indian Head to Ashland, a stretch of about thirty-five miles. How could they have covered that distance when they had no recollection of doing it?

Fourth, they had arrived home about two hours later than they should have. What had happened to those missing two hours?

Then they realized that the missing time and distance had occurred between the first time they heard the beeping and when they had finally heard it again. Had they both been asleep? Had the car driven itself?

Barney Hill had felt pains in his lower abdomen and upper thighs when he returned home. As time passed he became nervous and ill, suffering from ulcers and high blood pressure. Betty Hill had strange nightmares about UFOs.

Barney Hill consulted several doctors and only mentioned the UFO incident in passing. As he did not improve very much, he was finally told that perhaps he should undergo hypnosis. Both he and Betty Hill visited Dr. Benjamin Simon, a well-known neurosurgeon and hypnotherapist. (Neurosurgery is a branch of medicine dealing with surgery of nerve tissues; hypnotherapy is the treatment of disease by means of hypnosis.)

The story that emerged was astonishing! Neither could remember what had happened while they were awake but, when they were hypnotized, the events of that strange encounter with the UFO were quite clear in their minds.

After the first beeping, the Hills found that they were driving on a dirt road. They were stopped by a roadblock.

33

Some men took them through the woods to a large "saucer," which had landed. Betty Hill's eyes were open, but she said that her husband's eyes stayed closed all the time, and he moved as if he were walking in his sleep.

The men had broad, flat faces and large, slanting eyes which reached part way around their heads and seemed to give them extraordinary side vision. They had huge chests.

The leader of the crew seemed to have no lips, and his mouth was merely a slit. Nor did he appear to have a nose, just a couple of holes where normally a nose would be.

The Hills were taken aboard the ship and subjected to physical examinations. Betty Hill described hers in detail: A piece of fingernail was cut off, a sample of skin was scraped away, a hair was pulled out of her head. A long needle was inserted into her navel. The leader told her that it was a test to see if she were going to have a baby. When Betty Hill complained that the needle hurt, the leader simply passed his hand over her forehead and the pain stopped.

The examination showed that Barney Hill had false teeth, and this seemed to puzzle the humanoids. Betty Hill explained that sometimes people had to have their teeth removed when they were diseased, or when they grew old. The humanoids did not understand what "growing old" meant either.

Betty Hill said that she did not communicate with the leader by using words, but rather through exchanging thoughts. The only sound made by the humanoids was a kind of humming.

After the examination was over, the leader told Betty Hill that she would not be able to remember what had happened, and neither would her husband.

They were then released and allowed to go on their way. Nobody had really harmed them while they were aboard the spaceship.

34

After each trip to the hypnotist, Barney Hill's health seemed to improve. He wasn't nearly so nervous and he felt much better. His ulcers began to heal.

This is the strangest part of the story: Dr. Simon hypnotized Betty and Barney Hill separately. He kept tape recordings of what they said and did not tell either of them what the other had said while under deep hypnosis. Yet, *both stories were exactly the same!* It is very unlikely that stories could be made up while under hypnosis.

Were the stories true? Certainly Betty and Barney Hill believed them.

Betty and Barney Hill still live in Portsmouth, where she works for the New Hampshire state government as a social worker, and he works for the U.S. Post Office.

In September 1964, an attack by a robot was reported. It involved one of three hunters who drove into the mountains near Cisco Grove, California, to hunt deer with bows and arrows.

The hunters set out on foot together but separated when they reached a ridge, for they thought they might have better luck finding game that way.

One hunter, whom we shall call "Tom" (that is not his real name), walked along the ridge until he came to the edge of a cliff. Since there seemed to be no way to get down, he realized that he would have to walk back the way he had come.

He reached a canyon at about dusk. Suddenly, he heard a noise which sounded like a bear. Tom quickly climbed a large tree and stayed there until he was sure the animal had gone. Then he climbed down. Since it was getting dark and he feared he might get hopelessly lost if he went on alone, Tom built a few signal fires, hoping that someone would be attracted by them and come to his aid.

Presently, Tom saw a light coming toward him. As it moved

through the air, he thought it might be a rescue helicopter sent by his friends. However, when the light hovered nearby and there was no engine noise, Tom became frightened. He quickly climbed back into the tree, stopping on the lowest branch, which was about twelve feet off the ground.

The light circled around Tom's tree. There was a sudden bright flash, and he saw a large object with a dome, about four or five hundred yards away. It was dark in the canyon and Tom could not see too clearly.

He heard someone moving in the brush, and then a "man" appeared. Soon another man approached. Although Tom still could not see them clearly in the darkness, there was enough moonlight for him to ascertain that they were approximately five feet five inches tall and wore a kind of silver-gray coverall.

A little later they were joined by a third figure. This one did not seem to be a humanoid. The way it blundered through the brush, instead of walking around it as the others had done, seemed to indicate that it was a robot. It had red-orange lights where eyes should be and a mouth that dropped down when opened, to form a square hole.

The first two figures tried climbing the tree but failed. Then the robot shot gas at Tom from the hole in its mouth.

The gas did not make Tom unconscious, but he felt sick and almost lost his grip on the tree branch.

He started throwing things at the figures, such as his canteen, his shooting bow, and even the silver coins in his pocket. Then he lit pieces of his clothing and threw them at the figures. Each time the flaming bits of cloth came down, the figures would back away. In that manner several fires were started in the dry brush. Tom climbed higher in the tree and lashed himself to a branch with his belt.

Near dawn another robot joined the first one. They both

threw up clouds of gas at Tom, and now he did lose consciousness. Only his belt prevented him from falling.

When he awoke the figures were gone. Tom wore only a tee shirt, levis, shorts, socks and boots, having burned or thrown away his other clothing. He felt cold and tired.

He climbed down from the tree and started to walk back toward the camp. He lay down to rest from time to time and at last heard someone whistling. It was one of his friends searching for him.

Tom told the others what happened and they believed him. One of them, who had almost gotten lost himself, had also seen the bright, glowing light of the "spaceship" the previous night.

5

HOME BASE?

Let us imagine that everybody agrees the UFOs really are ships from space. Where could they have come from?

It would be a great relief to those who fear the possible arrival of creatures from outer space to learn that the UFOs originated on this planet, Earth, and were really just scientific experiments. But is this possible?

Only two nations on earth are powerful enough, or have the money, scientists, and materials necessary to create such flying objects: the United States and the Soviet Union. If one of them succeeded in building a craft which could move with tremendous speed and reverse directions without pausing, that nation would probably want to tell the rest of the world about it. After all, it would be a great propaganda victory. Such a secret could not be kept for long anyway. The United States tried to protect the secret of the atomic bomb, but the Soviet Union learned about it before many years had passed. And if the Soviet Union had perfected such a fantastic spaceship they would surely have boasted about it to the rest of the world, as they did when their first satellite, Sputnik I, was sent aloft.

Therefore, we can be fairly sure that the UFOs did not

come from earth. Several nations have sent up balloons (which have been mistaken for UFOs), weather satellites, and a variety of other space vehicles, but not spaceships.

Could the spaceships have come from any of the eight other planets in our solar system? How about Mercury or Venus?

The temperature on the side of Mercury that faces the sun is about 572 degrees Fahrenheit, while the side away from the sun is very cold. Furthermore, there appears to be very little, if any, atmosphere on Mercury.

As for Venus, in 1963 the Mariner II spacecraft sent out by the United States passed quite close to Venus and sent back a great deal of information about that planet that was new.

Venus seems to be covered by several layers of clouds, about forty or fifty miles deep. These heavy, dense clouds are almost like a steamy liquid. On the surface of Venus, below the cloud layers, the temperature is about 800 degrees Fahrenheit, which is hot enough to melt lead!

It is quite doubtful that humanoids, as described by those who have seen them, would be able to exist on Mercury or Venus. And if they could, they would certainly be unable to survive Earth's atmosphere or comparatively low temperatures, even with insulated spacesuits.

So it appears unlikely that the spaceships could have originated their journey from either Mercury or Venus.

Could the spaceships have come from the planet Mars?

In 1965, the Mariner IV spacecraft, also sent out by the United States, passed within six thousand miles of Mars and sent back a number of photographs.

These pictures show many craters on the surface of the planet, quite like those on the moon. The craters may have been there for a long time. If there were sufficient air and water on Mars, those craters would have been eroded and

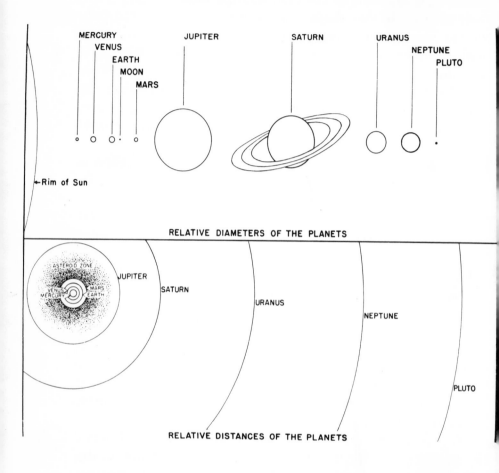

MERCURY
VENUS
EARTH
MOON
MARS
JUPITER
SATURN
URANUS
NEPTUNE
PLUTO

←Rim of Sun

RELATIVE DIAMETERS OF THE PLANETS

ASTEROID ZONE
JUPITER
VENUS
MERCURY
MARS
EARTH
SATURN
URANUS
NEPTUNE
PLUTO

RELATIVE DISTANCES OF THE PLANETS

This diagram compares the distances from the sun and sizes of the nine planets in our solar system.—*Hayden Planetarium*

smoothed over by atmospheric winds and water in a few thousand years. But nothing like that has happened.

It is possible that there is some water on Mars, but only in the form of ice. The ice seems to *sublimate* rather than melt. (Sublimation is the change of solid to gas, without first becoming a liquid.) The vapor passes right into what little atmosphere there is on Mars. Since scientists agree that the higher forms of life must have water in liquid form (not ice, not steam, but liquid) there is not much hope that humanoids exist on Mars.

Could the spaceships have come from Jupiter, Saturn, Uranus, or Neptune?

These planets are quite far from the life-giving sun. Jupiter, the largest planet in our solar system, is about 484,000,000 miles from the sun, while Neptune is 2,796,600,000 miles away from the sun. Therefore, it would be deadly cold on those planets. On Jupiter, the average temperature is about 211 degrees below zero Fahrenheit, while on Neptune, the surface temperature is approximately 328 degrees below zero.

The atmosphere on these planets seems to be composed mainly of methane and ammonia, which are poisonous to Earth humans.

Jupiter's atmosphere, according to scientists, is buffeted by violent storms. Its core may not be very solid. Saturn's atmosphere is so thick that it is almost like a fluid.

Uranus spins very rapidly on its axis. Although it takes eighty-four years for this planet to make one orbit around the sun (Earth, of course, takes only one year), one Uranus day lasts slightly less than eleven hours as time is figured on Earth.

All these conditions indicate that life on these planets probably does not exist, at least in the form of humanoids.

Could the spaceships have come from the planet Pluto? Scientists have been studying this planet for a number of years and have come to the conclusion that once Pluto was a satellite (a moon) of Neptune. Its orbit was changed when some unknown force drove it away from Neptune. Pluto now orbits around the sun.

Pluto is 3,670,000,000 miles from the sun, and consequently is probably the coldest body in our solar system. From scientific measurements it appears that there is very little atmosphere of any kind on Pluto. It would not be a habitable place for humanoids.

Thus it seems that if UFOs do exist they could not have come from any of the other planets in our solar system. No planet has the proper conditions to support the higher forms of life and, therefore, there is nobody on them to build or send out spaceships.

Is there any other place in the universe, outside the solar system, where such higher forms of life could exist?

A great many scientists say that the answer is—yes!

Our sun is simply a certain type of star. Looking up at the heavens on a clear night we can see many thousands of stars with the naked eye. If we look up with a telescope we can see vast numbers of additional stars. And there are a great many more stars that we can see if the most powerful kind of telescope it used.

The stars we see with the naked eye or with a small telescope form a group called a galaxy. Our sun is just one single star in the galaxy.

How many stars are there in this galaxy? Astronomers say that there are about *two hundred billion!* And they are spread out over a tremendous distance. How big a distance? It has to be measured in "light years."

Light travels at the rate of speed of 186,000 miles per second. In a year, a ray of light would travel approximately 5,880,000,000,000 (five trillion, eight hundred and eighty billion) miles. And, in order for that ray of light to travel from one end of our galaxy to the other, it would take 100,000 years! That is how big our galaxy is.

Furthermore, there are an unlimited number of galaxies in the universe. Some of the galaxies have only about ten billion stars, while others have even more stars than in our own galaxy.

Isn't it possible, then, that of all these billions upon billions of stars, some of them might have systems of planets similar to our own solar system?

Scientists say that there is every reason to believe there are many such stars, in our galaxy and in others. But in order to have a planet like our Earth, they must be the same type of star as our sun.

In that case, what kind of star is our sun?

All stars are not the same size. All stars do not have the same brightness. All stars do not give off the same amount of energy, such as heat, light, X-rays, etc.

Imagine that you are putting a poker into a very hot fire. As you watch, the poker begins to glow and becomes *red* hot. But if the poker is left in that hot fire, soon it will become even hotter. It will become *white* hot.

In a way the heat of stars is measured in similar fashion. We can determine how hot a star is by the color it gives off. Those stars which are the hottest seem to have a white or blue color. Those which are coolest are red (they are called "red stars").

Our sun is somewhere in the middle. It is considered "yellow." In a manner of speaking, when compared with other stars, it is not very hot nor very cool but just right. Our sun is called a "G-type star." Another star would probably also have to be a G-type in order to have a planet like Earth, which would have forms of life similar to Earth's.

Are there any stars in our galaxy which are G-type stars?

Once again, the answer is yes. There are probably many of them. One such star is named Beta Draconis. It is located in the constellation of Draco (a constellation is simply a grouping of some stars in the same region of the sky, as seen from Earth).

Beta Draconis is 310 light years away from our sun!

That means that if a spaceship could travel with the speed of light—186,000 miles per second—it would take 310 years for it to arrive on Earth.

Of course, we are not at all sure that Beta Draconis, or any other G-type star, really does have a system of planets. We can see the stars themselves, for they give off a good deal of light, as does our sun. But the planets cannot be seen, for they shine with weak reflected light, and you would have to be close to locate them, as planets give off no light of their own.

Distance is not the only difficulty the spaceship would have to overcome. Think of the fantastically powerful engines the craft would need, or the great length of time the engines would have to operate without using very much fuel. Think of the provisions that must be stored for the crew if they are humanoids. Think of the complicated navigational problems that would have to be solved in order to reach our solar system.

And there would be many dangers during the trip. The ship might suddenly be confronted with a swarm of meteoroids. It might go off course and be caught in the gravitational pull of another star. It might pass too close to a really massive star, which could burn through the heat shield of the spaceship.

Finally, it is very difficult to imagine any spaceship capable of traveling at a speed of 186,000 miles per second!

6

MASTERS OF THE STARS

Since scientists agree that a planet similar to our Earth might possibly exist if it is located near a star like our sun, then it is also possible that some higher form of life might exist on that planet. But they are not at all sure what that living creature would look like.

Dr. George Gaylord Simpson, a noted scientist in the field of evolution, does not believe in the idea of humanoids who look like Earthmen. He points out that the development of man took a long time and in some ways was an accident. The same accidents would have to happen in the same order on another planet, if a humanoid is to look anything like an Earthman.

Furthermore, says Dr. Simpson, even if those accidents should happen in another place, there might also be different accidents (the scientific term is mutations) which would develop other forms of life on other planets. For example, it is not impossible that a planet like our Earth would be ruled, not by a being like man, but by an insect, a shellfish, or some other type of creature. And there might be species of life on "the other Earth" which never developed on our Earth.

Other scientists do not agree with Dr. Simpson. Dr. Cyril Ponnamperuma, a research scientist with NASA (National

Aeronautics and Space Administration), says that any planet similar to Earth would have the same kind of biology-chemistry. If the other Earth was formed in the same way our Earth was formed, and if the same common and important elements of life were present, it is not at all impossible that evolution there would follow a course similar to Earth's. Dr. Ponnamperuma believes that creatures like man might very well exist somewhere in space.

Another expert in the field of evolution, Dr. R. Bieri, agrees with Dr. Ponnamperuma.

Taking these differences of opinion into consideration, let us try to figure out what kind of creature built those spaceships—if indeed spaceships do exist.

First, he would have to have a large, well-developed thinking center, or brain. This thinking center could not be of the same quality as that of lower forms of life. It would have to be capable of thinking, reasoning and solving problems that other species of life might not be able to solve.

Next, he would have to possess some sense organs. Probably the most important would be the ability to discern what is going on about him. It is possible that the creature would be able to see by means of a built-in radar system, like that of a bat. But, if he is building such a delicate and complicated mechanism as a spaceship, radar is not good enough. Eyes are better, for they allow one to judge depth, light, size—indeed, to know the difference between two objects which may be similar in appearance, but quite different in content. For instance, radar could not tell the difference between two books of the same size. But eyes would know instantly. And, since some humanoids in UFOs are described as having a kind of "wrap-around eyes," they would seem to have excellent vision, being able to see to the sides and front at the same

Sir John Herschel allegedly saw these lunar animals through his tele-scope in 1835.—*The Bettmann Archive, Inc.*

time. Perhaps humanoids might even have more than one pair of eyes.

Would such a creature have a nose? He could have, but it is not a necessity. A nose is used for breathing and to detect odors. A humanoid might breathe through the pores of his skin, or he could conceivably have some kind of antennae to detect odors. However, many higher forms of life do have noses of some sort.

The creature would probably have a mouth. Most living things have them, including some forms of vegetation, which use their leaves as a kind of "mouth" (the Venus flytrap and other plants of that type).

The humanoid would definitely have arms and fingers, for without them he could not grasp tools. It is the ability to grasp and manipulate various tools that has helped Earthman to reach such a high state of development.

How many arms and how many fingers would a humanoid have? The answer is, any amount. He could have two arms, or a dozen. He could have five fingers on each hand, or more. In fact the fingers might even be claws. It all depends on how the evolution of the creature progressed through the ages.

The humanoid is not a plant with roots in the soil. He is capable of movement, for if he were not, how could he board his spaceship?

He may have two legs, or he may have more. They may be shaped like an Earthman's legs, or have some other shape.

Actually, a humanoid might have more than one means of movement. He might have developed wings at some time in his evolution—or gills. The creature may be able to walk, fly and swim long distances underwater. However, the chances are that he can de *one* of these things best of all, and the others are merely additional, helpful ways for him to get from place to place.

He would need a body to store his vital organs. And he would have to have some supporting framework—bones.

There is reason to believe that through evolution he might have learned to stand erect, like Earthman.

Scientists think that Earthman really stopped being like an ape when he dropped down from the trees and then tried to stand erect to see if dangerous animals were nearby. This kind of posture also gave him two limbs which were not needed for walking, and the limbs became useful hands.

What would the creature eat? Perhaps he would feed on other forms of life, as Earth creatures do. But that is not necessarily so. This higher form of life might well have discovered how to make synthetic foods. But he certainly would have to drink water, or a similar liquid for, as was mentioned before, scientists think that life is not possible without some sort of liquid.

The humanoids on a distant planet might be taller than we are. It has been proved that Earthman has grown in physical stature since he discovered more facts about nutrition. From the size of suits of armor worn in medieval times, we know that modern man is about a foot taller than the knights of old. But he might not be as strong. Any creature who can invent a marvelous spaceship must also have invented many labor-saving devices and, in so doing, stopped using his muscles to do hard work. According to the theory of evolution, both man and the gorilla had the same ancestor. But man's brain developed, so now the gorilla is the stronger physically.

In a number of ways the life of the humanoid on another planet could be similar to the life of an Earthman. For example, since it would take many humanoids to build the spaceships, and since they would have to have a special place full of needed tools, there would probably be some kind of a factory. And because the humanoids would not want to waste time traveling great distances to and from the factory, they might live in cities or other communities.

If the humanoid did manage to make the trip to our planet, he might face grave danger from the bacteria in our atmosphere. He would not be immune to them, as we are.

Is it possible, then, that a humanoid might look like an Earthman? Perhaps. We cannot be sure until we see one! The science of *Exobiology* (living things outside our Earth) is so new that even the word Exobiology is not to be found in present dictionaries.

But one thing is certain: in order to build a spaceship capable of covering such vast distances and surmounting so many great obstacles, the humanoids would have to be far more intelligent than man on this planet Earth.

7

CONTACTING
OTHER PLANETS

Not very long ago astronomers could only study those stars
which could be seen through telescopes, spectroscopes, and a
few other instruments. Even with these, they managed to
learn a great deal about the heavenly bodies so very far away.

In 1932 an American electrical engineer named Karl G.
Jansky discovered that there was a great deal of radio energy
coming from outer space. He heard the energy in the form
of static. This static was traced to the stars.

Jansky's discovery interested other scientists and, in 1936,
another American engineer named Grote Reber invented a
special device which could investigate these faint radio waves.
That was the beginning of *radio astronomy.*

Through the use of these "radio telescopes," astronomers
have accumulated a great deal of new information about the
galaxies. Because the radio telescopes can penetrate into deep
space, even farther than an optical telescope, scientists have
been able to locate and analyze many more stars. But actually,
they do not see these distant stars, they "hear" them!

However, the sounds that come through the radio telescopes, although understandable to scientists, would seem like

Radio telescopes such as this one may enable us to communicate with
the inhabitants of other planets.—*UPI*

plain old radio static to anyone who was not scientifically trained.

Having found out that stars constantly emit this kind of radio noise, scientists began to wonder if radio waves might also be useful in trying to establish communication with planets that might be circling other stars. They wondered if there might be intelligent life on those planets—humanoids who could receive the signals sent from Earth. So powerful transmitters were built to send "messages" to other parts of the universe.

Of course they were not word messages. It would be ridiculous to transmit a message such as "Hello out there! Is anybody listening?" Aside from the obvious fact that the language used would not be understood, the power of the voice would "blur out" over long distances and would blend in with the natural static from our own sun.

But scientists realized that there was a way to contact someone in outer space, and that was through the use of mathematical signals. By sending *precise, repeated signals* over and over again, our scientists hoped that beings on other planets would realize that intelligent life was trying to contact them. In time, perhaps, the beings would be made to understand that the repetition of a regular pattern of signals was not merely natural static.

Of course, the scientists did not expect to receive a reply very soon. The signals they were sending were very weak by comparison with the natural radio noises emitted by the stars. And, even if those signals did manage to reach intelligent beings, it would take many years. Then they would have to allow time for the other beings to realize that intelligent life on our planet was sending the signals. More years would pass before their reply was received on Earth. And the humanoids would have to use precise, repeated signals in order to make themselves known and understood. Since the experiment was begun a comparatively short time ago, scientists did not expect anything except the radio noises they usually heard.

In 1967 British astronomers at Cambridge University were startled to hear *precise, repeated radio signals* on their radio telescopes.

These were "pulses"—rhythmic waves of radio energy—which were repeated with such precision that it seemed impossible that they were merely an accident of nature.

Each pulse lasted from thirty-eight to forty thousandths of a second, and the pulses, of varying lengths, were repeated at intervals of slightly more than one second. The signals were very powerful.

Puzzled astronomers began to formulate all sorts of theories. Was this a mathematical signal from outer space? Had someone out there thought of the same idea many years ago, and were they now trying to contact us by means of this pulsing signal?

Or, perhaps it wasn't a signal that meant "Hello out there!" Possibly it was a sort of navigational beam, similar to the navigational beams used by Earth airplanes to stay on course. If so, perhaps the signals came from spaceships.

Excitedly, the astronomers began trying to find out where the signals were coming from. And they succeeded! They traced the pulsings to an area about two hundred light years from our sun. They could not actually see a star in that spot, but they could hear it.

Still, some noted scientists have said that these pulsings are not from another civilization which is trying to establish contact with us. Nor are they navigational signals. They believe that the pulses come from a neutron star.

Although not too much is known about neutron stars, it is thought that they are formed when a large star burns up all its fuel. It then collapses and forms a more solid mass. This mass is not made up of ordinary atoms of material. Ordinary atoms contain electrons. The neutron star has no electrons left and is composed only of neutrons. The star shrinks in size. It may once have had a diameter of almost a million miles, but when the fuel is gone it becomes a solid chunk of material, perhaps a mere ten miles in diameter. The material of which the neutron star is composed is so heavy that a piece about the size of a golf ball would weigh many tons.

So perhaps the pulsing signals are not coming from intelligent life on a planet in outer space. Hopefully, in years to come, we will learn much more about this vast universe, of which we are only the tiniest part. Now we are like blind men, feeling our way uncertainly and trying our best to examine each unfamiliar thing we encounter.

The British astronomers who first discovered these pulsing signals have their own little joke about them. They call the strange radio waves "LGMs."

The letters stand for the words, "Little Green Men!"

8

IF YOU SEE A UFO

Perhaps, some day, you might see—or at least think you see —a UFO. If you do, study the object carefully, as long as you can keep it in sight. Try to remember as many details about it as possible. You will certainly want to tell others about what you have seen, and it is important that you do not forget anything.

The investigation of UFOs in America is the responsibility of the United States Air Force. They have instituted a program called "Project Blue Book." Officers collect reports and interview people who have sighted unidentified flying objects. They have already questioned a great many people who claim they have spotted UFOs.

In order to check and recheck all the facts of a sighting, the Air Force has prepared a printed questionnaire. Once it has been filled out, trained officers use the information for study and research. These are some of the facts they request:

Give your name, age, and home address.

Give the date and the time of the sighting.

Where were you when you saw the UFO? (town or city, the state).

How long was the UFO in sight?

These seem to be flying saucers, but are really the results of a defective camera lens.—*William Applewhite*

If the sighting took place during the day, was the sun shining?

If the sun was shining, was it behind you, to your left, your right, in front of you?

Were there clouds in the sky?

If the sighting took place during the night, were the moon and stars visible?

Did the UFO seem to be solid, or was it just a strange light in the sky?

Did the UFO seem to stand still for a time, or did it move constantly?

Did the UFO appear to change its shape at any time?

Did the UFO disappear suddenly, or did it speed away over the horizon?

Did the UFO move behind a cloud at any time?

Did you see the UFO with the naked eye, or through a telescope or binoculars?

Were you looking out the window of your home or automobile when you sighted the UFO?

Can you estimate the speed and altitude of the UFO?

Can you estimate how far away the UFO was from your position?

In which direction (north, east, south, west) was the UFO traveling?

Was anyone with you when you saw the UFO? If so, did that person see it too?

Was there more than one UFO?

Have you ever seen a UFO before? If so, was it in the same location as your present sighting?

Did you report the sighting to anyone?

All persons who believe they have sighted a UFO are urged to do the following:

First, think about it for a while. It is quite possible that you may find your own explanation for what you saw.

Next, if you are convinced that you *really* did see a UFO, report it to the nearest U.S. Air Force base. Each base has an investigator who follows up reports of UFO sightings.

If there is no Air Force base in your area, the report can be given to local police or state highway patrol officers. These officers may investigate the report, or they may turn over the information to the Air Force.

Happy sightings!

INDEX

Fort Knox, Kentucky, 11
Fort Scott, Kansas, 9
Fox-fire, 22
Fry, Daniel, 29

Galaxies, 42-43
Germany, 25
"Ghost blips," 21
Godman Air Force Base, Kentucky, 11-12
Gregory of Tours, 7
G-type star, 43-44

Hall, William, 16-18
Hamilton Steel Company (Hamilton, Ohio), 25
Hart, Carl, Jr., 20
Hill, Barney, 30-35
Hill, Betty, 30-35
Hillsdale, Michigan, 22
Hix, Guy, 11
Humanoids, 39, 41, 42, 53
  defined, 28
  described, 28-29, 30, 34, 36, 46
  experiences with, 29-37
  speech of, 39
  theories about, 45-50
  See also Robots
Hunt, David, 15-16
Hynek, Dr. J. Allen, 22-23
Hypnotherapy, 33, 35

Identified Flying Object, 24
IFO, 24
Indian Head, New Hampshire, 33
International Geophysical Year 1957-1958, 18
Interrupted Journey, The, 30

Iowa, sightings in, 23
Iowa State, 25

Jansky, Karl G., 51
Johnson, Fred, 11
Jupiter, 41

Klass, Philip, 25
Klem, Betty Jean, 16
Kubitschek, Juscelino, 18

"LGMs," 55
Light years, 42-43
Louisville, Kentucky, 11
Lubbock, Texas, 19-20
Luminous balls, 7-9

Madisonville, Kentucky, 11
Manitowoc, Wisconsin, 23
Mantell, Thomas, Jr., 11-12
Mariner II, 39
Mariner IV, 39
Mars, 30, 39-41
Mental telepathy with humanoids, 30, 34
Mercury, 39
Michigan, sightings in, 21-23
Milan, Michigan, 22
Milwaukee Astronomical Society, 24
Minneapolis, Minnesota, 23
Minnesota, sightings in, 23
Mongolia, sightings in, 9
Moon, 30
Mt. Rainier (Washington), 10
Muscarello, Norman, 14-16
Mutations, 45

National Aeronautics and Space Administration (NASA), 45
Nelson, Buck, 29-30
Neptune, 41, 42
Neurosurgery, 33
Neutron star, 54-55
New York City, 29
North Dakota, sightings in, 23
Northwestern University, 22

Oberg, Dr. A. G., 19-20
Ontario, Canada, sightings in, 23

P-51 fighter planes, 11
Ponnamperuma, Dr. Cyril, 45-46
Portsmouth, New Hampshire, 30, 32, 35
Pluto, 41-42
Presque Park Peninsula (Pennsylvania), 16-18
Pulsing signals from space, 54-55

Radar waves, 21
Radio astronomy, 51
Radio energy, 51, 54
"Radio telescopes," 51
Radio waves, 53
Reber, Grote, 51
Red stars, 43
Robinson, Dr. W. I., 19-20
Robots, 29, 35-37
Roerich, Nicholas, 9
Ruoff, Bert, 25
Russia, 23-24, 38

Saturn, 41
Schneider, Nuel, 22
Simon, Dr. Benjamin, 33, 35
Simpson, Dr. George Gaylord, 45

Socorro, New Mexico, 12
South Africa, 25
South Dakota, sightings in, 23
Space travel difficulties, 44
Sputnik I, 38
Sputnik IV, 23-24
Stars, 42-44
  heat of, 43
Sublimation, 41
Sun, 42-43
Swamp gas, 22-23

Temperature inversion, 21
Texas Tech, 19
Tibbetts, Douglas, 16-18
"Tom," experience of, with robots, 35-37
Tonopha, Nevada, Air Force Station, 24

UFOs
  in Bible, 7
  defined, 7
  early sightings of, 7-9
  explanations for, 20, 21, 22, 23-24
  investigation of, 56-59
  landings of, 7
  photographs of, 25
  possible sources of, 38-44
  practical jokes about, 25-27
  questionnaire about, 56-58
  recent sightings of, 10-18
  theories about, 9, 25
United States, 38
United States Air Force
  explanations for UFOs, 21
  investigations of UFOs, 56-59

63